FIFE'S LAST DAYS OF STI

by
W.A.C. Smith

The Forth Bridge, photographed from North Queensferry on 24 July 1952. Dwarfed by the massive cantilevers and barely visible through the latticework of girders class A3 Pacific no. 60089 'Felstead' crosses with the 2.15 p.m. express from Edinburgh (Waverley) to Aberdeen. The racehorse Felstead was winner of the 1928 Derby.

© W.A.C. Smith 2001
First published in the United Kingdom, 2001,
by Stenlake Publishing
Telephone / Fax: 01290 551122

ISBN 1 84033 179 8

All photographs by W.A.C. Smith

Rosyth estate at St Margaret's Bay on the north shore of the Firth of Forth was purchased by the Admiralty in 1903 for construction of a naval base to counter the threat posed by the rapidly expanding German High Seas Fleet. A station was opened within the dockyard early in the First World War for naval specials and workers' trains; in more peaceful times it was also to see excursionists for the annual Navy Days, and remains in situ although no longer in regular use. In the evening of 20 August 1959 class J35 0-6-0 no. 64496 comes under the main line and passes Naval Base Junction, where the dockyard line joined the old North Queensferry branch from Inverkeithing, with a workers' train for Edinburgh.

INTRODUCTION

The Kingdom of Fife was for many years the preserve of the North British Railway which, the largest of the Scottish companies with a route mileage of 1,378, had obtained Parliamentary powers in 1844 for construction of a line of railway from Edinburgh to Berwick-on-Tweed.

In later yeas the 'NB', as the company was familiarly known, was to form the Southern Scottish Area of the London & North Eastern Railway (1923) before becoming part of the Scottish Region of the nationalised British Railways (1948) while today it comes under the privatised Scotrail.

Some of the earliest coal workings in Scotland were in Fife and waggonways serving those included the Fordell Railway dating from about 1770 which ran from Crossgates to St David's Harbour on the Firth of Forth and survived (of 4' 4" gauge and latterly with steam haulage) until 1946. The Earl of Elgin's Railway originated in 1768 to reach the coast at Limekilns, and eventually extended to Charlestown Harbour. It was acquired by the NB in 1862, and received a passenger service in 1894. The Halbeath Railway was in existence from 1783 until 1867, with horse haulage for the conveyance of coals to Inverkeithing for shipment.

An important step forward was the opening of the Edinburgh & Northern Railway in 1847 which ran from Burntisland to Ferry-Port-on-Craig (later renamed Tayport) from where a ferry operated to Broughty Ferry on the Dundee side of the Tay. On the Forth there was a ferry between Granton and Burntisland carrying railway wagons and making it the world's first train ferry. It was designed by Thomas Bouch (the Edinburgh & Northern engineer) more often remembered for the first Tay Bridge which fell during a great storm at the end of 1879.

In 1849, the Edinburgh, Perth & Northern became the Edinburgh, Perth & Dundee, amalgamating with the North British in 1862. Fife was by now being served by railways which included the Stirling & Dunfermline, West of Fife Mineral, Kinross-shire, Fife & Kinross, Leven & East of Fife and St Andrews, all of these being acquired by the North British which, as late as 1906, completed the Kincardine loop and worked the Newburgh & North Fife Railway opened in 1909.

However, with the onslaught of road transport, closures commenced as early as 1926 and continued through the 30s into the 1950s, climaxing with the Beeching Report of 1963 which sealed the fate of the picturesque coast route, Tayport branch and Glenfarg main line, together with the line from Stirling to Alloa and Dunfermline, although there is a possibility of the latter being reinstated at some future date, while a survivor is the old Edinburgh & Northern branch from Ladybank to Perth. Also on the credit side has been the inauguration of the Fife Circle service and opening of new stations at Dalgety Bay and Glenrothes with Thornton, also Dunfermline Queen Margaret.

The second Tay Bridge was completed in 1887, and the North British route to Dundee and Aberdeen was firmly established by the opening of the Forth Bridge in 1890 with its connecting lines from Inverkeithing to Burntisland, Cowdenbeath to Kelty and from Mawcarse through Glenfarg to Bridge of Earn and into Perth. The nerve centres of the system were the strategically placed junctions at Inverkeithing, Dunfermline and Thornton which ensured that all attempts by the Caledonian Railway to penetrate the area were defeated.

The principal locomotive depots during the steam era were at Thornton and Dunfermline, and although diesel locomotives and multiple units had begun to infiltrate Fife in 1958 steam-hauled passenger trains did not disappear from the Kingdom until late in 1966. The summer of that year had seen what were thought to be the last such workings, but autumn brought a surprising comeback with two steam trains daily to and from Glasgow, this resulting from a DMU having been written off in an accident at Thornton motive power depot. These trains ceased after 5 November with closure of Glasgow's Buchanan Street Station, Fife services then reverting to Queen Street. On the penultimate day of operation B1 no. 61330 worked in with the 08.48 from Leven and no. 61407 took out the 11.35 for Thornton, this loco returning with the 16.45 from Kirkcaldy and the coaches then forming the 18.42 to Dunfermline with no. 61330.

As from 1 January 1967, BR steam locomotives in Fife were reduced to a total of sixteen (eleven at Thornton and five at Dunfermline) and all Scottish Region steam working ceased as from 1 May 1967.

A steam finale was, however, provided by the Wemyss Private Railway which dated from the turn of the century, connecting collieries with Methil docks. Despite linking BR and NCB lines it escaped nationalisation, but was closed in 1970 following a disastrous fire at the Michael Colliery at East Wemyss.

Fife was early in the field of railway preservation with the Lochty Railway opened in 1967, but this is now closed and dismantled. Currently, a railway preservation centre is proposed for Methil.

In August 1959 Class B1 4-6-0 no. 61148 heading the 2.15 p.m. train from Dundee to Edinburgh – which took a marathon four hours as it was routed via Crail and called at nearly every station en route – emerges from smoke-filled North Queensferry tunnel after the punishing 1 in 70 climb from Inverkeithing and draws to a stop in North Queensferry Station. Lights were installed in the tunnel after an accident in 1954 when a heavy sleeping car train slipped to a stand and then ran backwards, to be derailed at catch points, with the locomotive crew being unaware of what was happening.

Inverkeithing Central Junction, north of the station, was where the new line to Burntisland, for the opening of the Forth Bridge, diverged from the original Dunfermline to North Queensferry branch and where a spur from the East Junction to the North Junction formed a triangle. On 10 August 1957 D30 4-4-0 no. 62436 'Lord Glenverloch' approaches the station with the 5.56 p.m. from Dunfermline (Lower) which connected at Inverkeithing with services for Edinburgh, Glasgow and Thornton.

Post-war LNER Pacific no. 60532 'Blue Peter' of class A2 sweeps past Inverkeithing Central Junction on the main line with the 12.40 p.m. express from Aberdeen to Edinburgh on a hot and hazy August afternoon in 1959. This locomotive survives in preservation and has, indeed, passed this way in recent years with special trains. Lord Rosebery's 'Blue Peter' won the 1939 Derby and 2000 Guineas.

Another view of Inverkeithing Central Junction with B1 no. 61081 coming off the Dunfermline line with the 10.05 a.m. from Stirling to Edinburgh (Waverley) on 27 February 1960. The signal box was closed in 1980 upon opening of the Edinburgh Signalling Centre.

BR standard locomotives, the first of which appeared in 1951, were not much seen in Fife apart from several of the versatile class 4MT 2-6-0s shedded at Thornton. In February 1960 no. 76110 was photographed soon after leaving Rosyth (Halt) with the 11.35 a.m. from Dunfermline (Upper) to Edinburgh.

Rosyth (Halt) was opened during the First World War to serve a 'Garden City' housing staff at the dockyard and was later included in the public timetable. On 27 February 1960 B1 no. 61245 'Murray of Elibank' (this gentleman had been an LNER director) arrived with the 12.15 p.m. from Edinburgh to Cardenden.

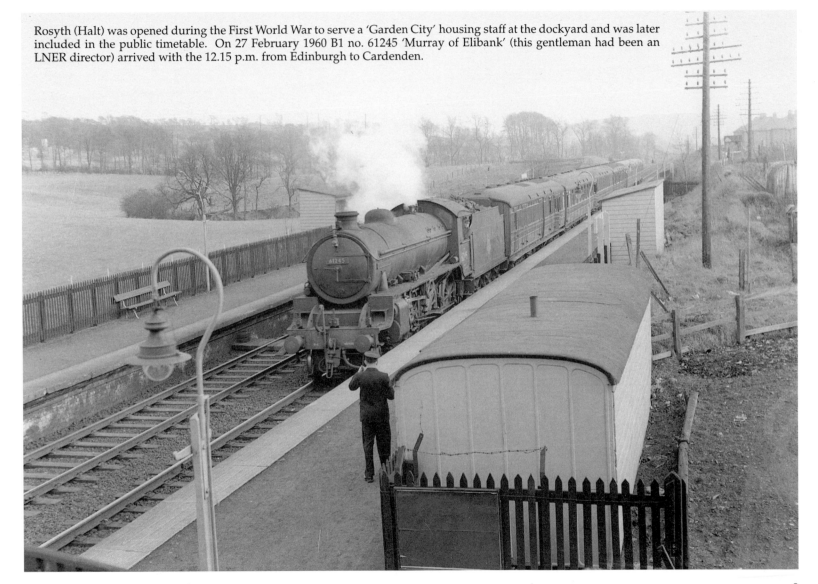

With a backdrop of derelict limekilns J35 0-6-0 no. 64525 poses for the camera at Charlestown, on the shores of the Firth of Forth, with the daily freight trip returning to Townhill Yard at Dunfermline, the train consisting of seven gunpowder vans from Crombie Naval Stores Depot. The photograph was taken on 26 December 1961, but the passenger service had ended 35 years earlier.

Dunfermline (Lower) from the north end on 20 April 1963 as the 10.03 a.m. train from Edinburgh to Perth via Glenfarg departs double headed by B1 no. 61076 and Black Five no. 45433.

B1 no. 61355 leaves Dunfermline (Lower) Station on 26 March 1960 with the 10.54 a.m. from Thornton Junction to Glasgow (Buchanan Street). Increasing train speeds required longer braking distances which meant that semaphore signal arms were sometimes carried on very tall posts to improve their visibility and with a repeater arm at the lower level as with this, the up starter, at Dunfermline where the signal arms are of the old North British Railway lower quadrant type.

Dunfermline Motive Power Depot was situated near to the Upper Station on the Stirling line and, in its heyday, housed some 70 locomotives. It was closed in 1967. Locomotives of the 0-6-0 wheel arrangement predominated, and on 26 March 1960 J36 nos. 65253 and 65239, J37 no. 64543 and J38 no. 65926 were in the shed yard.

Touch Junction allowed through running between the Upper and Lower Stations at Dunfermline while at nearby Townhill Junction the Thornton line was joined by that from Stirling and also by the erstwhile West of Fife Mineral Railway. On 25 May 1964 V2 2-6-2 no. 60836, one of the capable Green Arrow class introduced in 1936, approaches Townhill Junction with a freight from Edinburgh to Perth.

On 25 May 1964 'Austerity' 2-8-0 no. 90386, a former Ministry of Supply wartime built locomotive, passes Townhill Junction with an up empty wagon train.

A down freight hauled by J38 0-6-0 no. 65932 passes Lochgelly Station on 27 February 1960. There were 35 of these locomotives built by the LNER in 1926 for the Fife and Lothians coal traffic and they spent almost their entire working lives at Dunfermline, Thornton, Dundee and Edinburgh (St Margarets) sheds. This particular loco has been fitted with a small snowplough, a common practice at Scottish sheds during the winter months.

J38 no. 65905 hauls a railtour special past Westfield siding on the Lochore mineral line which ran from Redford Junction at Thornton New Yard through Kinglassie to Kelty. 19 June 1962.

Class 6P Jubilee 4-6-0 no. 45673 'Keppel', a former LMS loco, near Cowdenbeath North Junction on 27 February 1960 with the 2.05 p.m. express from Edinburgh to Perth.

On Boxing Day 1963 B1 no. 61072 leaves the Cowdenbeath line at Kelty South Junction and takes that for Lumphinnans North Junction with a coal train.

Class D49 4-4-0 no. 62712 'Morayshire' passing Lumphinnans Central Junction on 27 February 1960 with the 1.52 p.m. train from Thornton Junction to Dunfermline (Lower). The line going off on the left led to Kelty, being used by goods and mineral trains, while that on the right was the original route of the Dunfermline branch through Cowdenbeath (Old). 'Morayshire' has been preserved and is currently under overhaul by the Scottish Railway Preservation Society at Bo'ness in West Lothian.

Back to the East Coast main line, and class A2/3 Pacific no. 60519 'Honeyway' is seen passing Aberdour, a station renowned for its floral displays, with the 3.40 p.m. from Aberdeen to Edinburgh on 10 August 1957. 'Honeyway' was winner of the 1946 Champion Stakes.

On 24 July 1954 B1 no. 61064 leaves Burntisland with the 5.13 p.m. from Glasgow (Queen Street) to Thornton Junction and passes the 7¼ inch gauge locomotive 'Freda' on Dick's Miniature Railway, a temporary affair which operated on the links that summer.

The British Aluminium Co. works at Burntisland were established in 1915 alongside the main line, and a little to the east of the small Carron Harbour (site of the Newbigging limeworks waggonway of 1817), for the separation of alumina from imported bauxite ore and despatching of it, by rail, to plants at Fort William and Kinlochleven. On 26 October 1966 locomotive no. 1 (built by Peckett & Sons Ltd. of Bristol in 1915) was shunting.

On a dark, December day in 1959 B1 no. 61102 arrives at Dysart with the 12.19 p.m. train from Thornton Junction to Edinburgh. Dysart Station was opened by the Edinburgh & Northern Railway in 1847 and closed by British Railways in 1969. The signal box, however, remained in use for a further eleven years.

Thornton, on the E&N main line, became a junction in 1848 with the opening of a branch through Cardenden to Crossgates, this being extended to Dunfermline the following year. The Leven Railway followed in 1854 and the Buckhaven branch (later extended to Methil) was added in 1881 to make Thornton, with its miles of sidings for coal traffic, the railway crossroads of Fife. The station itself, a lengthy island platform with docks inset at either end and boasting a refreshment room for many years, required to be rebuilt on several occasions, and the permanent way needed constant packing with ash ballast, because of subsidence caused by colliery workings. On 23 May 1955 D11 4-4-0 no. 62675 'Colonel Gardiner' was pictured at the south end of the station with the 6.39 p.m. train to Glasgow (Queen Street Low Level). Closure came in 1969 and, with the tracks realigned, little trace remains.

At Thornton Junction the Methil train had its own platform, reached by a footbridge from the main station, and on a dreich 7 January 1955 (the day before withdrawal of the passenger service) D34 4-4-0 no. 62467 'Glenfinnan' was on the 2.40 p.m. departure. After closure, Methil saw occasional football specials until the relegation of East Fife FC.

J39 0-6-0 no. 64790 upon arrival at Thornton Junction on 1 July 1961 with the 5.49 p.m. from Anstruther. These locomotives were similar to the J38s, but larger diameter wheels made them more suitable for passenger trains.

At Thornton Junction passengers from the Anstruther train board the 5.31 p.m. from Broughty Ferry to Edinburgh. A3 Pacific no. 60098 carried the name 'Spion Kop' not in memory of the Boer War battle, but being that of a racehorse which won the Derby in 1920.

The class D49 4-4-0s were introduced by the LNER in 1927 and those bearing the names of counties were known as Shires (curiously, no engine was named 'Fifeshire') while others carried the names of hunts. None of the latter were allocated to Scotland until the early 1950s when Haymarket and Dundee MPDs received one each. That at Dundee was no. 62744 'The Holderness' (a hunt covering the Beverley and Driffield areas of Yorkshire) and it was photographed on 25 July 1959 while acting as station pilot at Thornton Junction. It was withdrawn from service some eighteen months later and scrapped.

Thornton shed on 28 August 1954 with D30 ex North British 4-4-0 no. 62442 'Simon Glover' (these locos carried the names of characters in the Sir Walter Scott novels), and J37 0-6-0 no. 64581. At this time the depot, built in 1933 to replace an earlier structure affected by subsidence, had an allocation of a hundred or more steam locomotives and had the shed code 62A.

J36 0-6-0 no. 65345 at Thornton shed on 15 October 1966 after filming of an episode of TV's *Dr Finlay's Casebook*. Built by the North British Railway at Cowlairs Works in 1900, and rebuilt in 1923, it was known to shed staff as the 'hill pilot' owing to its having been used to assist coal trains on the climb to Cowdenbeath. After a spell as a stationary boiler it was 'stored serviceable' at the shed together with no. 65288 (built in 1897) for possible use in a feature film and when officially withdrawn on 5 June 1967 these were the last steam engines in Scottish Region stock.

J38 0-6-0 no. 65910 awaits departure from Leslie on 16 August 1961 with the lightly loaded 4.10 p.m. freight over the 4¼ mile branch to the main line at Markinch, shunting as required at Auchmuty paper mill and Haig's whisky bottling plant. The passenger service over the branch had ended in 1932, freight surviving until 1967.

Auchtermuchty Station, opened by the Fife & Kinross Railway in 1857 and closed to passengers in 1950, was visited by an enthusiasts' special on 17 June 1960 with preserved North British 4-4-0 no. 256 'Glen Douglas' as motive power. Through working to Ladybank had ceased in 1957, this section being occupied by stored wagons, and the branch (from Mawcarse Junction on the Glenfarg line) was abandoned in 1964.

The Ladybank to Perth line through Newburgh was reduced to single track during the 1930s while in BR days the passenger service dwindled to two trains each way daily. On 23 May 1955 class 4P ex LMS compound 4-4-0 no. 40939 has arrived at Ladybank with the 4.10 p.m. from Perth.

Withdrawal of the service a few months later came as no surprise and the last train, on 17 September 1955 at 6.02 p.m. from Ladybank, was hauled by class 3P ex Caledonian Railway 4-4-0 no. 54494 pictured prior to departure. My belated thanks to driver G. Marshall of Perth for the footplate trip! Through trains returned to the line in 1975.

Back now to Thornton Junction where we find J37 0-6-0 no. 64618 arriving on 4 July 1959 with the 12.52 p.m. train from Crail which, on summer Saturdays, was extended to Edinburgh with a B1 in charge.

Cameron Bridge Station, situated between Thornton Junction and Leven, had an island platform which divided the adjoining distillery in two! On 22 March 1958, D34 4-4-0 no. 62478 'Glen Quoich' was starting away with the 10.12 a.m. from Inverkeithing to Anstruther.

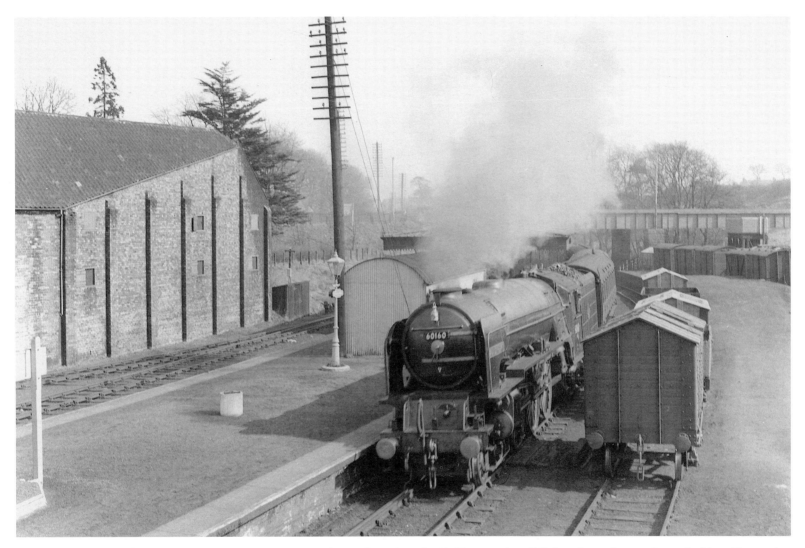

B1 4-6-0s were usually the largest locomotives seen at Leven, but on Saturdays the 12.47 p.m. train to Edinburgh was frequently worked by a Haymarket Pacific as on 22 March 1958 when A1 no. 60160 'Auld Reekie' was photographed at Cameron Bridge.

The chocolate coloured locomotives of the Wemyss Private Railway traversed a three mile system paralleling the BR Methil branch from West Wemyss and serving several collieries. On 12 June 1963 austerity 0-6-0 saddle tank no. 15 (built by Andrew Barclay & Co. at Kilmarnock in 1945) blasts through woodlands near Wemyss Castle with a loaded coal train.

J36 no. 65345 shunting at Montrave on 25 March 1961 with the freight trip from Thornton to Lochty. This remote branch, which never had a passenger service, was opened in 1898 as the East Fife Central Railway and, despite its grandiose title, terminated in a field at Lochty. An extension to Stravithie on the coast line never materialised and the branch was mainly used for seed potato traffic in winter and wagon storage in summer. It was closed in 1964. The loading gauge, seen on the right in the photograph, was to ensure that wagons once loaded did not foul lineside structures, overbridges or tunnels.

A visit to East Wemyss on 22 March 1958 had found 0-6-0T no. 19 (built by Barclay's in 1939) at the Wemyss Private Railway loco shed together with sundry wagons awaiting repair.

At Methil the Wemyss Private Railway met up with the National Coal Board at Wellesley Colliery and Denbeath Washer. On 19 April 1968 NCB 0-6-0T no. 8 posed for the camera in sidings adjoining the BR branch. This locomotive, built by Andrew Barclay & Co. in 1912, had been fitted with a Giesl exhaust ejector (named after its Austrian inventor) in place of a conventional chimney to improve boiler efficiency. NCB steam in Fife was to survive for a few more years at Comrie and Frances collieries, but no. 8 ended its working life at Bedlay Colliery in Lanarkshire.

From Leven the East of Fife Railway served Lundin Links, Largo, Kilconquhar, Elie, St Monance and Pittenweem before terminating at Anstruther in 1863 from where the line was extended through Crail to St Andrews, reached in 1887. At Lower Largo the Kiel Burn was crossed by a substantial arched viaduct seen on 25 July 1964 with B1 no. 61076 heading the 12.30 p.m. train from Crail to Edinburgh.

At Elie on 25 July 1959 class D34 4-4-0 no. 62478 'Glen Quoich' departs with the 12.52 p.m. from Crail to Edinburgh after making a crossing at the passing loop in the station (the coast line being single track) with the 9.37 a.m. from Glasgow (Queen Street) to Anstruther.

Temporarily promoted from its humdrum freight duties J37 0-6-0 no. 64616 was photographed near St Monance in July 1959 while working the 2.26 p.m. through train from Crail to Glasgow, although in all probability it would be replaced by a B1 at Thornton Junction.

A charming scene at St Monance during the golden summer of 1959 with appropriately named D30 4-4-0 no. 62418 'The Pirate' awaiting departure with the 3.12 p.m. train to Thornton Junction. A sparkling blue sea, station garden a riot of colour, camping coach in a siding for happy holidaymakers and smartly turned out locomotive typify the Fife coast line as I like to remember it, a line which even had its own named train, 'The Fife Coast Express'.

A surprising sight at Pittenweem on 25 July 1959 was class 5MT 2-6-0 no. 42737 with the 1.20 p.m. train from Edinburgh (Waverley) to Crail. These rather odd looking former LMS locos, nicknamed Crabs, were more at home in the Ayrshire coalfield than on the Fife coast, although this particular example was shedded at Grangemouth.

J37 0-6-0 no. 64602 leaving Anstruther for Thornton Junction with an enthusiasts' special from Dundee on 1 May 1965. In the background on the right can be seen the platform of the original terminal station.

There was a small engine shed at Anstruther, dating from its days as a terminus, and although the shed was eventually closed by British Railways the turntable remained. On 4 September 1965, penultimate day of passenger services on the coast line, B1 4-6-0 no. 61344 was turned after working the 13.18 train (as per the newly adopted 24 hour clock) from Edinburgh to Crail.

This was the last passenger train to traverse the coast line. On 25 June 1966 J37 0-6-0s no. 64570 and 64618 leave Thornton Junction for Anstruther, 1¼ hours late at 17.15, with a marathon railtour which had commenced at London (Waterloo) the previous night (and was returning overnight from Aberdeen!) utilising a variety of locomotives. The J37s had taken over at Edinburgh.

A fairly frequent service was operated between Leuchars Junction and St Andrews and on 9 August 1958 C16 ex NB 4-4-2T no. 67501 was on the 1.26 p.m. departure. Unfortunately, this useful link was to be wantonly destroyed like so much of our railway heritage.

The Newport Railway connected Tayport with the south end of the Tay Bridge at Wormit and enjoyed a considerable commuter traffic for Dundee until the coming of the road bridge brought closure of the railway in 1969. In happier times standard 2-6-4T no. 80123 calls at Newport-on-Tay (East) with the 5.47 p.m. from Tayport to Dundee. 23 May 1963.